DK WORKBOOKS

K Language Arts

Author Anne Flounders

DK

LONDON, NEW YORK, MUNICH,
MELBOURNE, and DELHI

US Editor Margaret Parrish
Editor Camilla Gersh
Managing Art Editor Richard Czapnik
Art Director Martin Wilson
Preproduction Editor Francesca Wardell

DK Delhi
Editor Rohini Deb
Assistant Art Editor Radhika Kapoor
Art Editor Jyotsna Julka
DTP Designer Anita Yadav
Deputy Managing Editor Soma B. Chowdhury

First American Edition, 2014
Published in the United States by DK Publishing
4th floor, 345 Hudson Street, New York, New York 10014

15 16 17 18 10 9 8 7 6 5 4 3 2
002-196481-03/14

Copyright © 2014 Dorling Kindersley Limited

A catalog record for this book
is available from the Library of Congress
ISBN: 978-1-4654-1737-4

DK books are available at special discounts when purchased in bulk
for sales promotions, premiums, fund-raising, or educational use.
For details, contact:
DK Publishing Special Markets
4th floor, 345 Hudson Street, New York, New York 10014
SpecialSales@dk.com.

Printed and bound in China

All images © Dorling Kindersley Limited
For further information see: www.dkimages.com

Discover more at
www.dk.com

Contents

This chart lists all the topics in the book. Once you have completed each page, stick a star in the correct box below.

FACTS

Lowercase letters are the small letters.
The first letters of the alphabet are **a** through **n**.

Trace lowercase letters **a** through **n**.
Then write these letters in lowercase on your own.

a a a a art	h h h h ham
b b b b bad	i i i i ill
c c c c cat	j j j j jet
d d d d dot	k k k k kit
e e e e egg	l l l l lot
f f f f fit	m m m m mad
g g g g get	n n n n not

The letters in most words are in lowercase.
The last letters of the alphabet are **o** through **z**.

Trace lowercase letters **o** through **z**.
Then write these letters in lowercase on your own.

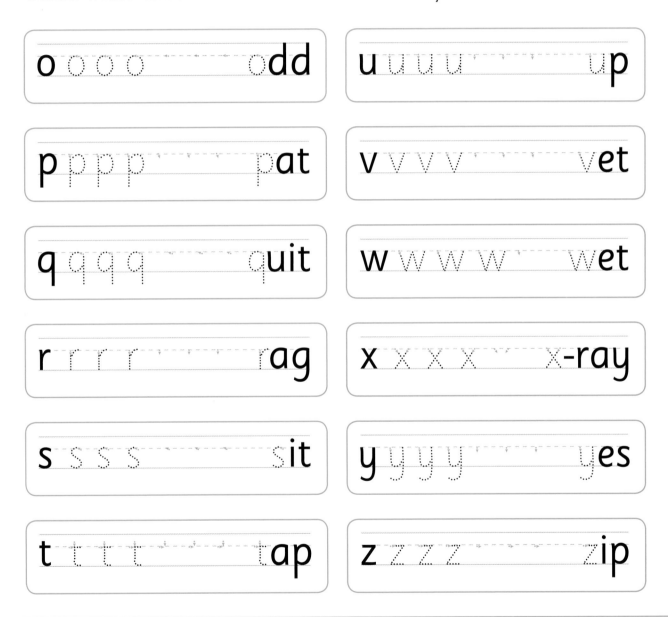

o o o o odd	u u u u up
p p p p pat	v v v v vet
q q q q quit	w w w w wet
r r r r rag	x x x x x-ray
s s s s sit	y y y y yes
t t t t tap	z z z z zip

Can you think of some words beginning with
the letters **a** through **z**?

Uppercase letters are used in the names of people, places, or events. These are the letters **A** through **N** in uppercase.

Practice writing the uppercase letters. First trace the letters. Then write uppercase letters **A** through **N** on your own.

A A A   April

H H H Hannah

 B B B   Brad

I I I I   Ivan

C C C   Cody

 J J J   Joe

D D D   Dan

 K K K   Kim

E E E E Easter

L L L   Logan

 F F F   Fred

M M M Morgan

 G G G   Grace

 N N N   Nora

Uppercase letters are used at the beginning of a sentence and in titles. Here are the letters **O** through **Z** in uppercase.

Practice writing the uppercase letters. First trace the letters. Then write uppercase letters **O** through **Z** on your own.

O O O   Owen

U U U   Uma

P P P   Paul

V V V   Vic

Q Q Q   Quinn

W W W   Will

R R R   Randy

X X X   Xavier

S S S   Sam

Y Y Y   Yoko

T T T   Tom

Z Z Z   Zach

Can you think of some names beginning with the letters **A** through **Z**?

FACTS

Books have covers. Covers give information about books.

Description	Instruction
The title is the name of the book.	Look at the book's cover. Draw a box around the title.
The author is the person who wrote the book.	Draw a line under the author's name.
A book title uses uppercase letters. People's names also start with uppercase letters.	Circle all the uppercase letters.
The title and picture on a book's cover can give you a clue as to what the book will be about.	What do you think you would read in this book? Finally, color the book cover.

Silly Skunk Stories

Rosy **S**niffin

Stories have a beginning, a middle, and an end.

Look at the pictures below. Then tell the story they show aloud. What happens first? What happens next? What happens last? When you have told the story, color the pictures.

1.

2.

3.

4.

FACTS

The letter **a** can sound like the **a** in "apple" (short "a") or the **a** in "ape" (long "a").

Each word is missing its short "a." Write the letter to complete the word. Then read each word aloud.

w_g

b_t

s_d

c_p

f_n

g_s

Two words that end in the same sound are called rhyming words. Rhyming words begin with different sounds.

Read the sentences aloud. Draw a line under the rhyming words.

My dad was mad.

A mat is flat.

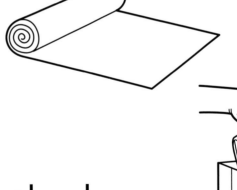

Put the rag in the bag.

The rat sat on the cap.

FACTS

Rhyming words often have similar spellings. Sometimes rhyming words can have completely different spellings.

Read each word aloud. Find the pairs of rhyming words in the balloons. Color each pair the same color.

A nursery rhyme is a poem or song for children.
Nursery rhymes are passed down through the years.

Read the nursery rhyme aloud. Underline the rhyming words.
Draw a picture that illustrates the nursery rhyme.

Hey, diddle, diddle,
The cat and the fiddle,
The cow jumped over the Moon.
The little dog laughed
To see such sport,
And the dish ran away with the spoon.

Saying words aloud can make it easier to figure out if they rhyme. Here are some more rhyming words to practice.

Find the rhyming words to practice. Draw a line between each pair.

book

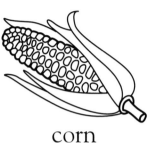

corn

clock

hook

horn

socks

fox

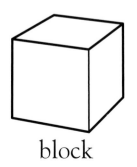

block

Complete the Sentences

Some words are used often in reading and writing.
You can learn to recognize these words.

Read the words aloud. Use them to complete sentences.

off	out	from	in	to	for

I gave the bag _____ Bob.

The gift is _____ you.

Jane took the book _____ me.

The dog is _____ the house.

We are _____ of the car.

The lid is _____ the pot.

FACTS

A character is a person or animal in a story.

Read the story aloud.

> A wolf liked to look at the stars. One night,
> he walked along looking up at the stars.
> He didn't see a hole in the ground and fell into it.
> Another wolf passing by said, "You see the stars far
> away. Why don't you see the ground under your feet?"

Below, circle the character that this story is about.

A setting is where and when a story takes place.

Read the story aloud.

Jenny and Jack climbed on a sled. They zoomed down a hill. The winter air turned their cheeks cold. The sled stopped at the bottom of the hill.
Jack said, "Let's ride again!"

Circle the picture that shows the setting of the story.

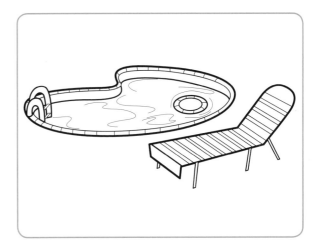

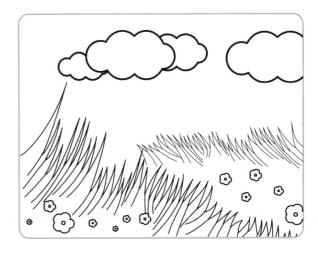

FACTS

The letter **e** can sound like the **e** in "egg"
(short "e") or the **e** in "eel" (long "e").

Each word is missing its short "e." Write the letter
to complete the word. Then read each word aloud.

j_t

h_n

b_d

w_b

p_t

l_g

Rhyming words in a sentence make it more fun to read. Here are some more rhyming words.

Read the sentences aloud. Draw lines under the rhyming words.

I led the red hen.

She fed the wet pet.

A bird can rest in a nest.

Ten men saw the pen.

People read for different reasons.
Sometimes they read to learn.

Read the text below.

> A map helps you find your way. A map can show
> your home. It can show your school. A map can
> show you how to go from your home to your school.

Circle the picture that shows what the text is about.

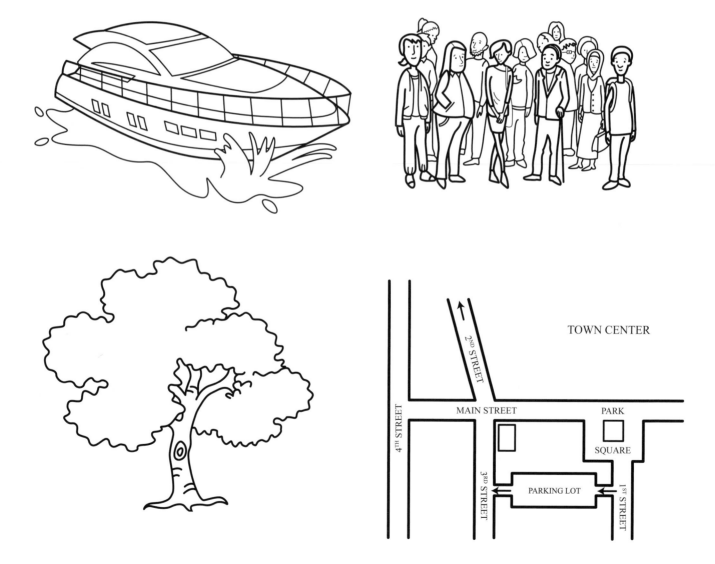

Labels are a text feature.
They give information about a picture.

Write labels naming the parts of the tiger.
Use the words from the word bank.

| back | ear | eye | leg | nose | tail |

FACTS

A noun names a person, a place, or a thing.

Circle the words that are nouns.

bird

run

train

man

pull

leaf

car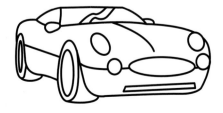

book

A verb is an action word. It names anything one can do or be.

Circle the words that are verbs.

Sun

kick

jump

door

hide

sing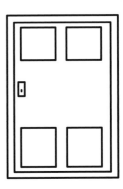

frog

hold

FACTS

The letter **i** can sound like the **i** in "big" (short "i") or the **i** in "ripe" (long "i").

Each word is missing its short "i." Write the letter to complete the word. Then read each word aloud.

d_g

k_d

s_t

r_p

b_b

p_n

One way to create a word that rhymes with another word is to change the first letter of the word.

Make rhyming words using letters from the letter bank.

| r | d | w | p | f | t |

_in   _in

_id   _id

_ig   _ig

Adjectives are words that describe people, places, or things.

Draw a line between the picture and
the word that describes it.

funny

red

soft

loud

Telling or writing information in order helps it make sense.

This story is out of order. What happens first, next, and last? Write 1, 2, and 3 by the pictures to put them in the correct order.

Make sense of information by telling
or writing it in order.

Read the text below. Then look at the pictures.
Number the pictures 1, 2, 3, and 4 to show
the order in which the story happened.

Meg wanted to sell lemonade. First, she made the lemonade.
Next, she set up her stand. Then, she hung up a sign.
Finally, Meg sold lots of lemonade to her friends!

The letter **o** can sound like the **o** in "dog" (short "o") or the **o** in "rope" (long "o").

Each word is missing its short "o." Write the letter to complete the word. Then read each word aloud.

p_t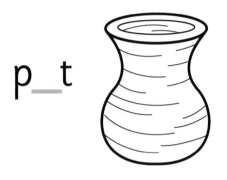

d_t

fr_g

s__ck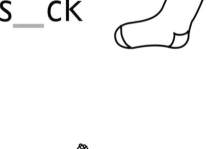

m_p

r_d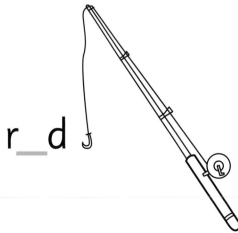

FACTS

If words end with the same sound, they are rhyming words.

Read the sentences aloud. Circle the rhyming words.

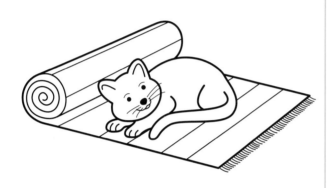

The cat sits on the mat.

Bob likes corn on the cob.

Lots of dogs sit on logs.

The pot is not too hot.

Words can name a general idea or topic, such as "place" or "job." Other words are more specific, such as "city" or "teacher."

Find the words that name foods in the spaces. Color those spaces red. Find the words that name animals in the spaces. Color those spaces green.

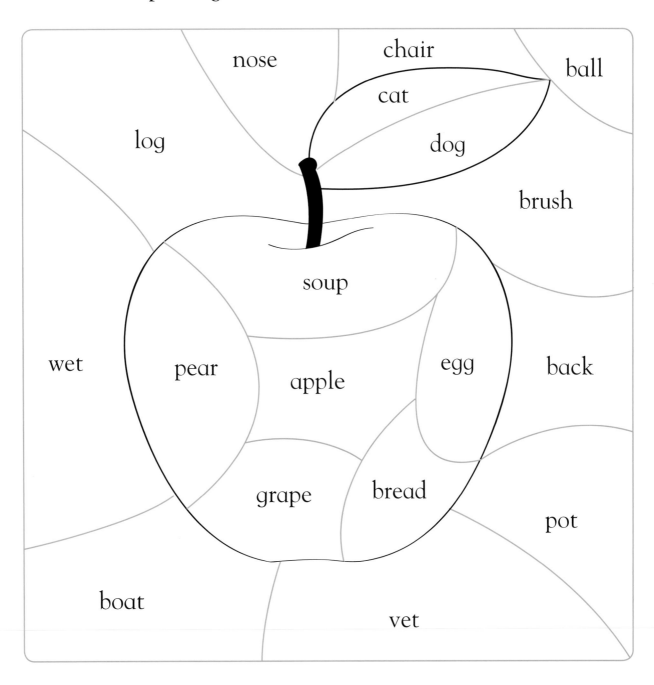

FACTS

Singular means one. Plural means more than one. To make some words plural, add an **s** at the end of the word.

Make these words plural.

bat_

pig_

cane_

pan_

Add **es** to make a plural of words that ends in **ch**, **sh**, **s**, or **x**.

Make these words plural.

fox__

dish__

match__

dress__

A story has a title, or name. Stories are made up by authors. Stories also have characters and a setting.

Write down the title, author, characters, and setting of your favorite storybook. Write down why you like it.

My Favorite Storybook

Title: ....

Author: ....

Characters: ....

Setting: ....

Why I like this book: ....

....

Draw a picture of something that happens in your favorite storybook.

My Favorite True Book

Books about true events are called nonfiction books. Nonfiction books can inform us about a subject.

Write down the title, author, and subject of your favorite true book. Write down why you like it.

My Favorite True Book

Title: ....

Author: ....

Subject: ....

Why I like this book: ....

....

....

Draw a picture of what your favorite true book is about.

FACTS

The letter **u** can sound like the **u** in "up" (short "u") or the **u** in "use" (long "u").

Each word is missing its short "u." Write the letter to complete the word. Then read each word aloud.

r_g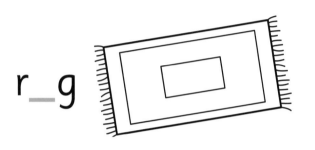

b_d

h_t

c_b

b_s

p_p

Using a rhyme in a sentence can make it easier to remember.

Read the sentences aloud. Draw lines under the rhyming words.

It is fun to run.

Can you cut a nut?

A bug is on the mug.

The fox is in the box.

Some words sound alike but are spelled differently. These are called homophones.

Read each pair of words aloud. They sound alike! Trace the letters that change the spelling of the words.

te a   te e

s o n   S u n

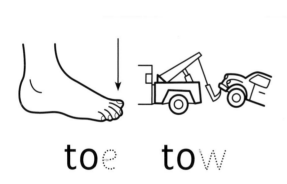

to e   to w

Fairy Tale

ta i l   ta l e

ha i r   ha r e

bl ew   bl ue

This popular song names different parts of the body.

Sing or say the song. As you sing, point to the parts named. Then use words from the song to label the parts of the body.

Head, shoulders, knees and toes, knees and toes.
Head, shoulders, knees and toes, knees and toes.
And eyes, and ears and mouth and nose.
Head, shoulders, knees, and toes, knees and toes.

Question words help people think about and understand what they read, do, or see.

The animals are running a race in the park. Look at the picture. Then answer the questions.

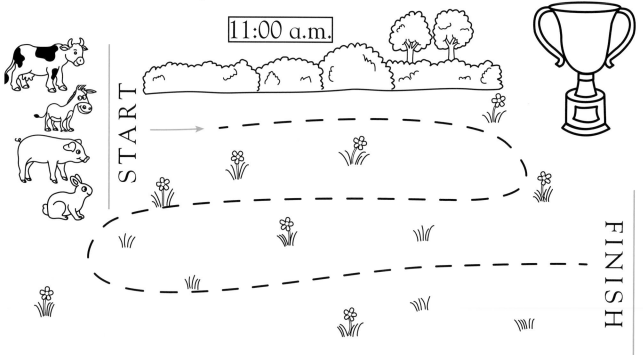

Who is running the race? Circle the answer in the picture.

What will the winner of the race get? Draw a box around it.

Where will the runners go? Trace the answer with your pencil.

When is the race? Circle the answer.

Why do you think the race is in a park? Talk about your ideas.

How will the runners know where to go? Draw a box around the answer.

Question words are words that help people ask for information.

Select question words from the word bank to best complete each question.

who	what	where	when	why	how

.... do you tie a shoe?

.... is at the door?

.... are there clouds in the sky?

.... is my dog?

.... will we eat dinner?

.... time is it?

FACTS

Letters are used together to make new sounds.
These letters are called blends.

Use the letters from the word bank to
complete each word. Say the words aloud.

| bl | br | cl | cr | gl | gr |

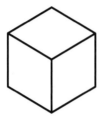

__ock

__ue

__ips

__apes

__ush

__ab

Certain letters make special sounds when they are used together.

C + H makes the sound that starts the word "chip."
S + H makes the sound that starts the word "sheep."
T + H makes the sound that starts the word "thin."
Draw a line to connect each word to its sound.

shoes

 TH

chair

cheese

SH

think

three

CH

ship

FACTS

Sometimes one word has more than one meaning.
Some words are both nouns and verbs.

Use the words in the word bank to write
the names of the pictures.

| box | duck | fall | train |

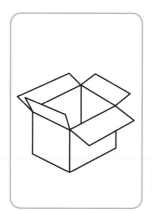 

....

....

Every letter has an uppercase and a lowercase form.

For each letter, fill in the missing uppercase
or lowercase letter.

a	B	C	d
e	f	g	H
I	j	K	L
m	n	o	P
q	r	s	T
u	V	w	X
y	Z		

Some words are easy to recognize.
Others need to be sounded out.

Say the words describing these pictures aloud.
Then write the words.

....

....

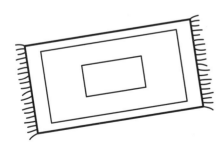

....

People can share ideas and give information through writing.

Complete the sentences to describe your day.

My Day

My name is ....

Here is what happened to me today/yesterday. (Circle one.)

First, ...

....

Then, ...

....

Finally, ...

....

I felt ....

.... !

Certificate

Congratulations to

....

for successfully
finishing this book.

GOOD JOB!

You're a star.

Date

....

Answer Section with Parents' Notes

This workbook is a fun way to help your child build kindergarten literacy skills. All of the activities support the Common Core English Language Arts Standards, a set of shared educational goals for each grade level currently used by 45 states, the District of Columbia, and four U.S. territories.

Contents

These activities are intended for a child to complete with adult support. These topics will help children understand the world of words around them:

- writing the letters of the alphabet;
- uppercase and lowercase letters;
- short vowel sounds;
- consonant blends;
- sight words;
- rhyming words;
- sound-alike words;
- ordering events using temporal words;
- forming plurals with **-s** and **-es**;
- nouns, verbs, and adjectives;
- question words;
- story characters;
- story settings;
- text features;
- reading for personal enjoyment.

How to Help Your Child

On each page, read the facts and instructions aloud. Provide support while your child completes the activity. Encourage questions and reinforce observations to build confidence and increase participation at school.

Throughout the workbook, children will learn how to decode short CVC (consonant-vowel-consonant) words. This will help them recognize these words as they read and later on help them with longer words, too.

As you work through the pages, help your child connect the content to specific personal experiences. For example, as you read a book together, explore the book cover. Ask your child to retell a story you have read, using temporal words such as "first," "next," "then," and "finally." Practice writing skills by writing short letters to family and friends or by labeling pictures your child has drawn.

Be sure to praise progress made as a page is completed, a correct answer is selected, or a thoughtful response is given. This will help build the child's confidence and enjoyment in learning. Above all, have fun!

★ The Lowercase Alphabet

FACTS

Lowercase letters are the small letters.
The first letters of the alphabet are **a** through **n**.

Trace lowercase letters **a** through **n**.
Then write these letters in lowercase on your own.

a a a a a a a art	h h h h h h h ham
b b b b b b b bad	i i i i i i i ill
c c c c c c c cat	j j j j j j j jet
d d d d d d d dot	k k k k k k k kit
e e e e e e e egg	l l l l l l l lot
f f f f f f f fit	m m m m m mad
g g g g g g g get	n n n n n n n not

Children can also practice writing other simple three-letter words in lowercase letters. Help them think of words that begin with **a** through **n**.

5

The Lowercase Alphabet ★

FACTS

The letters in most words are in lowercase.
The last letters of the alphabet are **o** through **z**.

Trace lowercase letters **o** through **z**.
Then write these letters in lowercase on your own.

o o o o o o o odd	u u u u u u u up
p p p p p p p pat	v v v v v v v vet
q q q q q q q quit	w w w w w w wet
r r r r r r r rag	x x x x x x-ray
s s s s s s s sit	y y y y y y y yes
t t t t t t t tap	z z z z z z z zip

Can you think of some words beginning with the letters **a** through **z**?

Have your child look in books for short, simple words starting with **o** through **z** and set in lowercase. Children can copy the words and name the letters as they write. Read the words with your child.

6

★ The Uppercase Alphabet

FACTS

Uppercase letters are used in the names of people, places, or events. These are the letters **A** through **N** in uppercase.

Practice writing the uppercase letters. First trace the letters.
Then write uppercase letters **A** through **N** on your own.

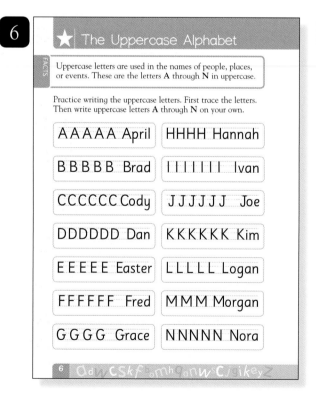

A A A A A April	H H H H Hannah
B B B B B Brad	I I I I I I I Ivan
C C C C C C Cody	J J J J J J Joe
D D D D D D Dan	K K K K K K Kim
E E E E E Easter	L L L L L Logan
F F F F F F Fred	M M M Morgan
G G G G Grace	N N N N N Nora

Invite children to write their first, middle, and last names with correct capitalization.

The Uppercase Alphabet ★

FACTS

Uppercase letters are used at the beginning of a sentence and in titles. Here are the letters **O** through **Z** in uppercase.

Practice writing the uppercase letters. First trace the letters.
Then write uppercase letters **O** through **Z** on your own.

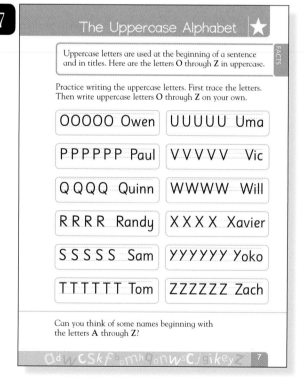

O O O O O Owen	U U U U U Uma
P P P P P P Paul	V V V V V Vic
Q Q Q Q Quinn	W W W W Will
R R R R Randy	X X X X Xavier
S S S S S Sam	Y Y Y Y Y Yoko
T T T T T T Tom	Z Z Z Z Z Z Zach

Can you think of some names beginning with the letters **A** through **Z**?

Continue to practice uppercase writing by writing the name of your street and city.

★ Book Time

FACTS

Books have covers. Covers give information about books.

Description	Instruction
The title is the name of the book.	Look at the book's cover. Draw a box around the title.
The author is the person who wrote the book.	Draw a line under the author's name.
A book title uses uppercase letters. People's names also start with uppercase letters.	Circle all the uppercase letters.
The title and picture on a book's cover can give you a clue as to what the book will be about.	What do you think you would read in this book? Finally, color the book cover.

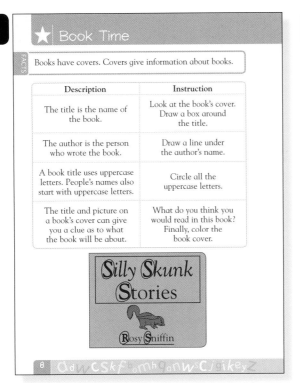

When you read books with your children, point out the features on the cover: title, author, and illustrator. Invite children to make predictions about the story based on the information on the cover. If the book is a familiar one, talk about why the cover illustration is (or is not) a good choice for the book.

9

Tell a Story ★

FACTS

Stories have a beginning, a middle, and an end.

Look at the pictures below. Then tell the story they show aloud. What happens first? What happens next? What happens last? When you have told the story, color the pictures.
Answers may vary

1. A skunk picked some flowers in the forest.

2. A dog wandered into the forest.

3. The skunk was afraid of the dog.

4. The skunk offered the dog flowers. They became friends.

After reading books to children, invite them to retell what happens first, next, and at the end.

10

★ Short "a"

FACTS

The letter a can sound like the a in "apple" (short "a") or the a in "ape" (long "a").

Each word is missing its short "a." Write the letter to complete the word. Then read each word aloud.

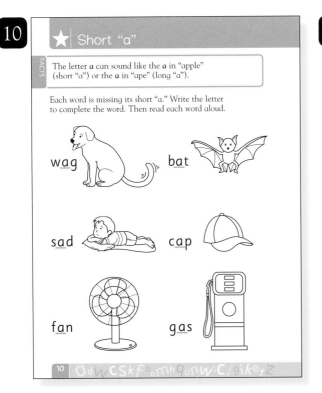

wag   bat

sad   cap

fan   gas

Find simple words in books that have an a. Read them with your child and ask if the word has a short "a" or long "a."

11

Rhyming Words ★

FACTS

Two words that end in the same sound are called rhyming words. Rhyming words begin with different sounds.

Read the sentences aloud. Draw a line under the rhyming words.

My <u>dad</u> was <u>mad</u>.

A <u>mat</u> is <u>flat</u>.

Put the <u>rag</u> in the <u>bag</u>.

The <u>rat</u> <u>sat</u> on the cap.

Encourage your child to think of other short "a" rhymes. Offer help in writing them down.

★ Rhyming Match

FACTS

Rhyming words often have similar spellings. Sometimes rhyming words can have completely different spellings.

Read each word aloud. Find the pairs of rhyming words in the balloons. Color each pair the same color.

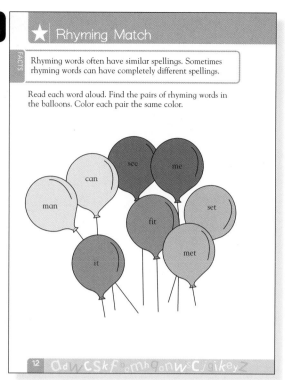

see   me
can
man   set
fit
it   met

Invite your child to name other words that rhyme with the words in the balloons. Write them on the page.

Nursery Rhymes ★

FACTS

A nursery rhyme is a poem or song for children. Nursery rhymes are passed down through the years.

Read the nursery rhyme aloud. Underline the rhyming words. Draw a picture that illustrates the nursery rhyme.

Hey, <u>diddle</u>, <u>diddle</u>,
The cat and the <u>fiddle</u>,
The cow jumped over the <u>Moon</u>.
The little dog laughed
To see such sport,
And the dish ran away with the <u>spoon</u>.
Drawings may vary

What other nursery rhymes do you know? Repeat this activity with other favorites.

★ Spot the Rhymes

FACTS

Saying words aloud can make it easier to figure out if they rhyme. Here are some more rhyming words to practice.

Find the rhyming words to practice. Draw a line between each pair.

book   corn

clock   hook

horn   socks

fox   block

Point out that although "fox" and "socks" rhyme, they do not end with the same letters.

Complete the Sentences ★

FACTS

Some words are used often in reading and writing. You can learn to recognize these words.

Read the words aloud. Use them to complete sentences.

| off | out | from | in | to | for |

I gave the bag ___to___ Bob.

The gift is ___for___ you.

Jane took the book ___from___ me.

The dog is ___in___ the house.

We are ___out___ of the car.

The lid is ___off___ the pot.

Look online for your school or district's list of kindergarten high-frequency words (or sight words).

16

★ Story Characters

FACTS | A character is a person or animal in a story.

Read the story aloud.

A wolf liked to look at the stars. One night,
he walked along looking up at the stars.
He didn't see a hole in the ground and fell into it.
Another wolf passing by said, "You see the stars far
away. Why don't you see the ground under your feet?"

Below, circle the character that this story is about.

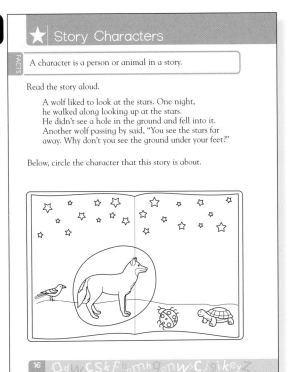

Invite your child to name and describe favorite
characters from well-known stories.

17

Story Setting ★

A setting is where and when a story takes place. | FACTS

Read the story aloud.

Jenny and Jack climbed on a sled. They zoomed
down a hill. The winter air turned their cheeks cold.
The sled stopped at the bottom of the hill.
Jack said, "Let's ride again!"

Circle the picture that shows the setting of the story.

As you read books to your child, point out details
about the setting. Talk about how the setting
adds to the story.

18

★ Short "e"

FACTS | The letter e can sound like the e in "egg"
(short "e") or the e in "eel" (long "e").

Each word is missing its short "e." Write the letter
to complete the word. Then read each word aloud.

jet   hen

bed   web

pet   leg

Find simple words in books that have an e.
Read them with your child and ask if the word
has a short "e" or a long "e."

Rhyming Words ★

Rhyming words in a sentence make it more fun
to read. Here are some more rhyming words. | FACTS

Read the sentences aloud. Draw lines under
the rhyming words.

I led the red hen.

She fed the wet pet.

A bird can rest in a nest.

Ten men saw the pen.

Encourage your child to think of other short "e"
rhymes. Help your child write them.

★ Information

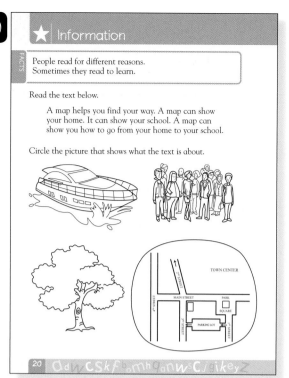

People read for different reasons.
Sometimes they read to learn.

Read the text below.

A map helps you find your way. A map can show your home. It can show your school. A map can show you how to go from your home to your school.

Circle the picture that shows what the text is about.

Describe examples of things you read to learn: for example, newspapers, cookbooks, and instructions.

Labels ★

Labels are a text feature.
They give information about a picture.

Write labels naming the parts of the tiger.
Use the words from the word bank.

back   ear   eye   leg   nose   tail

ear   eye   back   tail   nose   leg

Look for examples of labels in texts around your home. Point them out to your child.

★ Spot the Nouns

A noun names a person, a place, or a thing.

Circle the words that are nouns.

bird   run   train   man   pull   leaf   car   book

Ask your child to name other nouns. Search for things that are nouns in the place where you are sitting.

Spot the Verbs ★

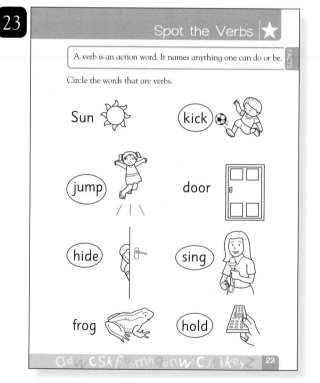

A verb is an action word. It names anything one can do or be.

Circle the words that are verbs.

Sun   kick   jump   door   hide   sing   frog   hold

Invite your child to name other verbs. Your child can act out different verbs and name them, for instance, "dance," "skip," and "wiggle."

★ Short "i"

FACTS

The letter **i** can sound like the **i** in "big" (short "i") or the **i** in "ripe" (long "i").

Each word is missing its short "i." Write the letter to complete the word. Then read each word aloud.

d i g   k i d

s i t   r i p

b i b   p i n

Find simple words in books that have an i. Read them with your child and ask your child if the word has a short "i" or long "i."

Rhyming Words ★

FACTS

One way to create a word that rhymes with another word is to change the first letter of the word.

Make rhyming words using letters from the letter bank.

Answers may vary

r	d	w	p	f	t

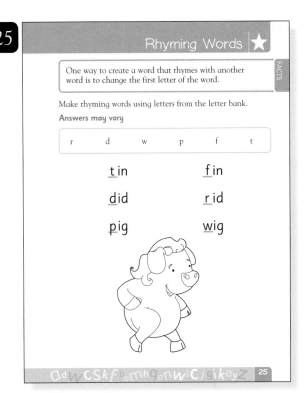

t in   f in
d id   r id
p ig   wig

Encourage your child to think of other short "i" rhyming words. Offer help when writing the words.

★ Spot the Adjectives

FACTS

Adjectives are words that describe people, places, or things.

Draw a line between the picture and the word that describes it.

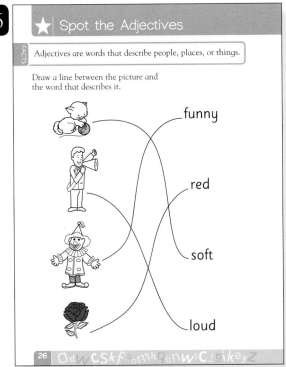

funny

red

soft

loud

Ask your child to name other adjectives. Use adjectives to describe the things you see around you.

First, Next, Last ★

FACTS

Telling or writing information in order helps it make sense.

This story is out of order. What happens first, next, and last? Write 1, 2, and 3 by the pictures to put them in the correct order.

Words that convey time and order are called temporal words. Ask your child to retell other stories using words such as "first," "second," "next," "then," "finally," and "last."

★ Ordering Events

Make sense of information by telling
or writing it in order.

Read the text below. Then look at the pictures.
Number the pictures 1, 2, 3, and 4 to show
the order in which the story happened.

Meg wanted to sell lemonade. First, she made the lemonade.
Next, she set up her stand. Then, she hung up a sign.
Finally, Meg sold lots of lemonade to her friends!

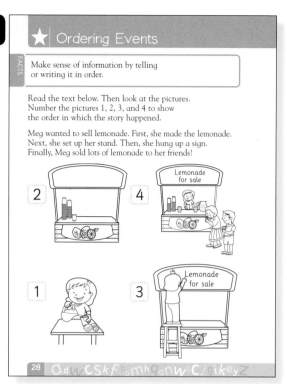

Have your child retell the story in order using
temporal words.

Short "o" ★

The letter **o** can sound like the **o** in "dog"
(short "o") or the **o** in "rope" (long "o").

Each word is missing its short "o." Write the letter
to complete the word. Then read each word aloud.

pot

dot ●

frog

so ck

mop

rod

Find simple words in books that have an **o**.
Read them with your child and ask your child
if the word has a short "o" or long "o."

★ Rhyming Words

If words end with the same sound, they are
rhyming words.

Read the sentences aloud. Circle the rhyming words.

The (cat) sits
on the (mat).

(Bob) likes corn
on the (cob).

Lots of (dogs)
sit on (logs).

The (pot) is
(not) too (hot).

While you read the sentences aloud, invite
your child to point to other words that have
a short "o" sound, even if they don't rhyme.
For instance, "on," "lots," and "of."

Sorting ★

Words can name a general idea or topic, such as "place" or
"job." Other words are more specific, such as "city" or "teacher."

Find the words that name foods in the spaces. Color those
spaces red. Find the words that name animals in the spaces.
Color those spaces green.

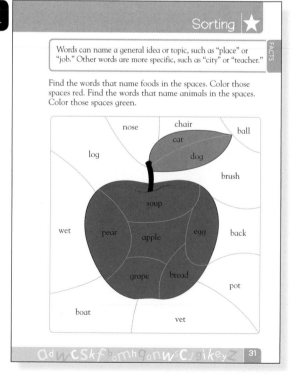

Collect some objects from around the house that
have a similar theme: for example, toys and tools.
Have your child sort and group the items and
name the word that describes each group.

★ Plurals Add **s**

FACTS

Singular means one. Plural means more than one. To make some words plural, add an **s** at the end of the word.

Make these words plural.

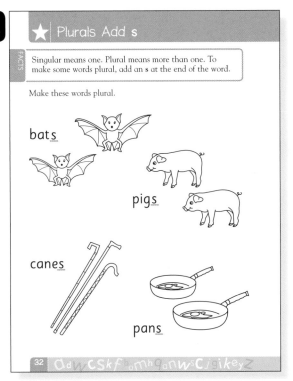

bat**s**

pig**s**

cane**s**

pan**s**

Brainstorm other words that can be made plural with an -**s**.

Plurals Add **es** ★

FACTS

Add **es** to make a plural of words that ends in **ch**, **sh**, **s**, or **x**.

Make these words plural.

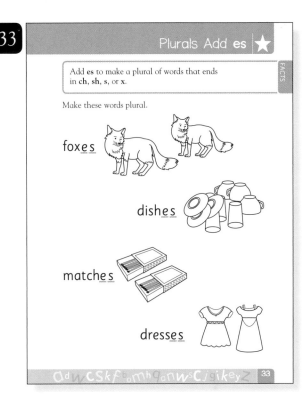

foxe**s**

dishe**s**

matche**s**

dresse**s**

Brainstorm other words that can be made plural with an -**es**.

★ My Favorite Storybook

FACTS

A story has a title, or name. Stories are made up by authors. Stories also have characters and a setting.

Write down the title, author, characters, and setting of your favorite storybook. Write down why you like it.

My Favorite Storybook

Title: **Answers may vary**

Author: **Answers may vary**

Characters: **Answers may vary**

Setting: **Answers may vary**

Why I like this book: **Answers may vary**

Draw a picture of something that happens in your favorite storybook.

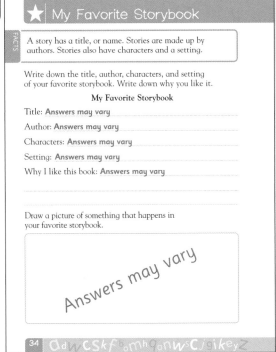

Answers may vary

If your child has several favorite books, repeat the activity on separate pieces of paper.

My Favorite True Book ★

FACTS

Books about true events are called nonfiction books. Nonfiction books can inform us about a subject.

Write down the title, author, and subject of your favorite true book. Write down why you like it.

My Favorite True Book

Title: **Answers may vary**

Author: **Answers may vary**

Subject: **Answers may vary**

Why I like this book: **Answers may vary**

Draw a picture of what your favorite true book is about.

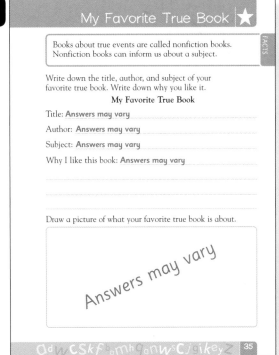

Answers may vary

If your child has several favorite books, repeat the activity on separate pieces of paper.

★ Short "u"

FACTS

The letter **u** can sound like the **u** in "up" (short "u") or the **u** in "use" (long "u").

Each word is missing its short "u." Write the letter to complete the word. Then read each word aloud.

rug

bud

hut

cub

bus

pup

Find simple words in books that have a **u**. Read them with your child and ask your child if the word has a short "u" or long "u."

Rhyming Words ★

FACTS

Using a rhyme in a sentence can make it easier to remember.

Read the sentences aloud. Draw lines under the rhyming words.

It is <u>fun</u> to <u>run</u>.

Can you <u>cut</u> a <u>nut</u>?

A <u>bug</u> is on the <u>mug</u>.

The <u>fox</u> is in the <u>box</u>.

Encourage your child to think of other short "u" rhymes. Offer help in writing them. Also encourage your child to point out other short vowel sounds, such as the short "a" in "can" or the short "o" in "on."

★ Sound-Alike Words

FACTS

Some words sound alike but are spelled differently. These are called homophones.

Read each pair of words aloud. They sound alike! Trace the letters that change the spelling of the words.

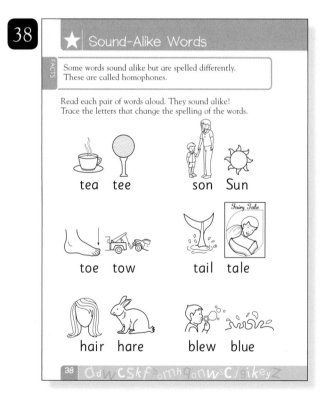

tea   tee   son   Sun

toe   tow   tail   tale

hair   hare   blew   blue

Words that sound alike are called homophones. "Homo" means "same" and "phone" means "sound." What other homophones can you and your child think of?

Action Song ★

FACTS

This popular song names different parts of the body.

Sing or say the song. As you sing, point to the parts named. Then use words from the song to label the parts of the body.

Head, shoulders, knees and toes, knees and toes.
Head, shoulders, knees and toes, knees and toes.
And eyes, and ears and mouth and nose.
Head, shoulders, knees, and toes, knees and toes.

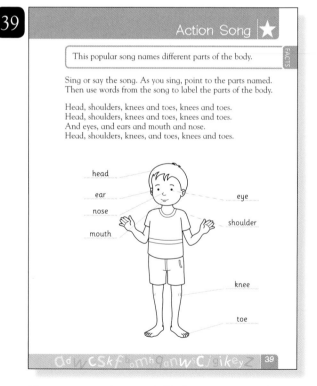

head
ear
nose
mouth
eye
shoulder
knee
toe

If you can, teach your child the movements that go with this song. This will make the song easier to remember.

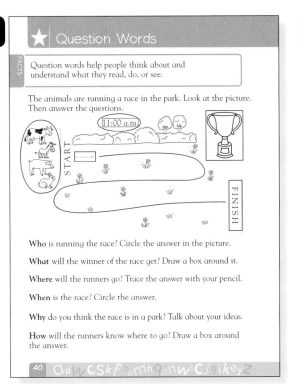

⭐ Question Words

FACTS

Question words help people think about and understand what they read, do, or see.

The animals are running a race in the park. Look at the picture. Then answer the questions.

11:00 a.m.

START

FINISH

Who is running the race? Circle the answer in the picture.

What will the winner of the race get? Draw a box around it.

Where will the runners go? Trace the answer with your pencil.

When is the race? Circle the answer.

Why do you think the race is in a park? Talk about your ideas.

How will the runners know where to go? Draw a box around the answer.

Here, children are invited to explain why they think the race is in a park. Answers will vary; there are no wrong answers. This is a good opportunity for children to think critically. For example, is running in a park safer than running in the streets? Maybe traffic would have been tied up if roads were closed for a run.

Question Words ⭐

FACTS

Question words are words that help people ask for information.

Select question words from the word bank to best complete each question. **Answers may vary**

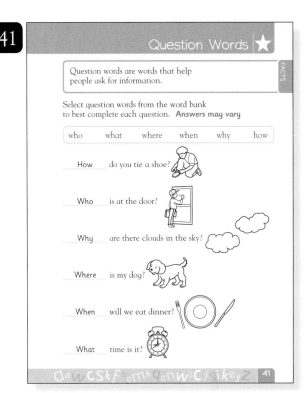

| who | what | where | when | why | how |

How   do you tie a shoe?

Who   is at the door?

Why   are there clouds in the sky?

Where   is my dog?

When   will we eat dinner?

What   time is it?

Be sure to encourage your child to write the letters with correct capitalization. Words that begin a sentence start with an uppercase letter.

⭐ Consonant Blends

FACTS

Letters are used together to make new sounds. These letters are called blends.

Use the letters from the word bank to complete each word. Say the words aloud.

| bl | br | cl | cr | gl | gr |

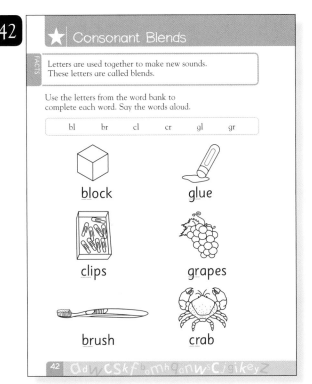

block   glue

clips   grapes

brush   crab

Encourage your child to think of other words with the **bl**, **br**, **cl**, **cr**, **gl**, and **gr** consonant blends.

Consonant Blends ⭐

FACTS

Certain letters make special sounds when they are used together.

C + H makes the sound that starts the word "chip."
S + H makes the sound that starts the word "sheep."
T + H makes the sound that starts the word "thin."
Draw a line to connect each word to its sound.

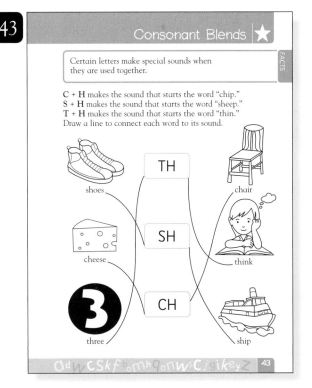

shoes   TH   chair

cheese   SH   think

three   CH   ship

Have your child keep an eye out for signs around town that have the **ch**, **sh**, and **th** consonant blends. Point them out as you see them and read them aloud.

★ Nouns and Verbs

FACTS

Sometimes one word has more than one meaning.
Some words are both nouns and verbs.

Use the words in the word bank to write
the names of the pictures.

| box | duck | fall | train |

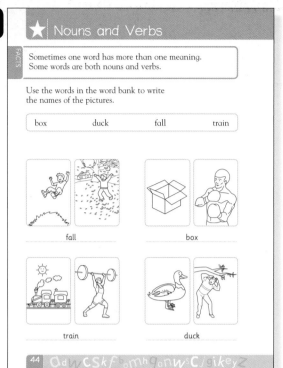

fall

box

train

duck

As you read or converse with your children, keep
eyes and ears open for other words that work as
nouns and verbs (for example, "walk," "shower,"
and "hook").

Handwriting Letters ★

FACTS

Every letter has an uppercase and a lowercase form.

For each letter, fill in the missing uppercase
or lowercase letter.

A a	B b	C c	D d
E e	F f	G g	H h
I i	J j	K k	L l
M m	N n	O o	P p
Q q	R r	S s	T t
U u	V v	W w	X x
y Y	Z z		

For extra practice, have children write
their names and complete address.

★ Handwriting Words

FACTS

Some words are easy to recognize.
Others need to be sounded out.

Say the words describing these pictures aloud.
Then write the words.

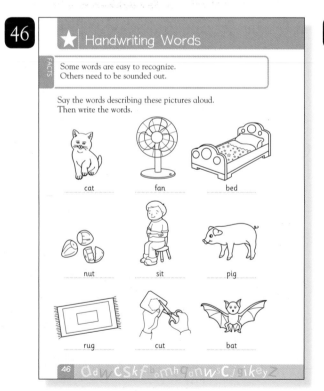

cat

fan

bed

nut

sit

pig

rug

cut

bat

For extra practice, invite children to write
a note to a grandparent or have them help
write a grocery list.

Write About It ★

FACTS

People can share ideas and give information
through writing.

Complete the sentences to describe your day.

My Day

My name is **Answers may vary** .

Here is what happened to me today/yesterday. (Circle one.)

First, **Answers may vary**

Then, **Answers may vary**

Finally, **Answers may vary**

I felt **Answers may vary**

!

This activity can be repeated regularly on
separate pieces of paper. Tell your child that
writing daily about one's thoughts and experiences
is called keeping a journal. At this age, children
may not want to take on a daily journal, but using
this activity as a template for regular practice can
build writing skills.